With His
Hand In Yours

With His Hand In Yours

An Everyday Pilgrim's Answers
To Coping Every Day
Of The Year

Phyllis Hobe

The C. R. Gibson Company
Norwalk, Ct. 06856

Copyright © 1985 by Guideposts Associates, Inc.
Carmel, New York 10512
Published by The C. R. Gibson Company
Norwalk, Ct. 06856
Printed in the United States of America
ISBN 0-8378-5074-6

Illustrations by Judith Fast
Text design by Holly Johnson at The Angelica Design Group, Ltd.

Grateful appreciation is expressed to Guideposts Associates, Inc. for permission to adapt and excerpt material in this volume that originally appeared in COPING—A GUIDEPOSTS BOOK FOR CHRISTIAN LIVING TODAY published and copyrighted by Guideposts in 1983.

Contents

Introduction

When I gave my life to Christ, I thought He was going to change it. He didn't. He changed *me*. And *that* made a difference in my life.

Is it better? Yes. But not easier.

Am I happy? Infinitely. But happiness is not what I once thought it would be.

How is my life different? It isn't mine; it's His, and it took some time for me to understand what that means. I had to learn that only by giving myself could I receive Jesus Christ.

And my faith? What happened to it? I'm living it. With Christ's help. With His love. With His presence. And with His assurance that whatever I can't do, He can.

I am not perfect. I continue to make mistakes and He continues to forgive me. Sometimes, when I find it difficult to walk with Him, I go my own way. I always come back and He always welcomes me.

Every now and then I succeed in giving Him so much of my obedience that I feel His thoughts in my own mind. I see with His eyes. His strength enables me to do what I never believed was possible. For some brief moments I have been able to love as He loves. It has been the greatest blessing I have ever known.

Meeting life as a Christian does not mean we will avoid problems. We will know ups and downs, we will confront hard decisions and unexpected changes. We are not immune from stress and the ravages of anxiety. New experiences will come our way and we will not always know what to do about them. We will hold joy close to us and hope it will last forever; we will weep when it does not. We will share our lives with many, and when some bonds are broken we will know pain that does not end. We are so very human.

But we are more than that. Coping with the complexities of life is only the beginning of our story, and we will go on from there. Because for the Christians there is a beyond. It's the discipleship that grows out of the coping; it's the giving of ourselves to others, that brings us closer to God. That is our goal.

And there are steps along the way to that goal. They will take us through challenges that demand more courage, insight, under-standing, love and suffering than we have. That is how we will discover the incredible power God is waiting to give us every day of our lives.

Phyllis Nobe

Ministering To
Your Inner Needs

Fear thou not; for I am with thee: be not dismayed; for I am thy
God: I will strengthen thee; yea, I will help thee.
Isa. 41:10

> *And to him that knocketh it shall be opened.*
> Lk. 11:10

God opens many doors to us—and sometimes I wish He wouldn't. I find it difficult trying to decide which one He wants me to enter.

I also wish God would open some doors that insist on remaining closed in spite of all my attempts to push them open. I like to think I have a right to go where I choose.

Such is the dilemma of a disciple. What does God want for us? And why don't we always want the same things?

"I refuse to believe that God wants me to go through the rest of my life as a blind woman!" Ginny said, her mouth tightening in a hard line. She was twenty-three, pretty, and very much alone in the world. Now a door had closed in her face, the door of sight. She had been examined by specialists, all of whom agreed she would be totally blind in another year. They didn't know why. And there was no cure.

"What will I do?" Ginny said. "I've already had to give up my job. What kind of work can a blind person do? How will I live? How can I earn some money?"

They were enormous questions and they would have to be considered one at a time. Blind men and women *do* earn a living. Financial aid is available to them for emergencies and special education. But Ginny would have none of that kind of talk.

She knew better. She would pray. She would take God at His

word and *insist* on His help. She would knock at that closed door until it opened and she could see again.

She prayed. She went to more doctors. She ate foods and took vitamins said to improve vision—which might have worked if Ginny had any vision left. But she didn't. In less than a year she was totally blind. I lost touch with her when she moved out of her apartment and left no forwarding address. It was as if she had been swallowed up by her own darkness.

Then I saw her again a few years later. She came toward me, walking along a busy city street filled with shoppers and office workers on their lunch hour. I stopped, amazed. She was more beautiful than ever and she walked with her head held high and there was a smile on her face. Alongside her, fitted with a special harness, was a large dog, a guide dog, maneuvering her briskly along the crowded sidewalk.

She stopped when I called her name and we threw our arms around each other. We had to talk hurriedly because Ginny was on her way to class. She was teaching Braille to adults who had recently lost their sight.

"I was depressed for a long time," she told me. "That's why I moved away. I tried to move away from God, too, because I was mad at Him. Then I realized that He didn't do this to me. He was hurting just as much as I was because I couldn't see. So I asked Him if there was something else I could do besides see. That's when I began to accept the fact that I was blind. I learned how to walk with a cane, and then I decided a guide dog could help me move even more. When I tackled Braille, though, I ran into a problem. It's awfully hard to learn. So the harder I tried, the more I wanted to teach other people how to read with their fingers. That's what I'm doing now—and I have to run or I'll be late for class!"

A door had closed. And another had opened.

Ginny wasn't wrong to fight for her sight when she learned she was losing it. Sometimes we have to be like Jacob and wrestle with God. It strengthens our faith: *"I will not let thee go, except thou bless me"* (Gen. 32:26. KJV). Or we must dare to speak with the honesty of the father who brought his son to Christ for healing. The boy had been unable to hear and speak since childhood and, obviously, specialists had been consulted. As a last resort, perhaps, the father had brought his son to Christ's disciples—and they couldn't heal him. Now he knocked again at a closed door. *"Oh, have mercy on us and do something if you can,"* he said to Jesus (Mk. 9:22, Living Bible).

Not a great statement of faith, was it? But very much like our prayers of desperation. Full of *maybe's* and *if's* and *I'll try anything, Lord!*

"If I can?" Jesus asked. *"Anything* is possible if you have faith" (v. 23). And we can imagine God saying that to us more often than we care to admit. Doubt has a way of perforating our faith.

And then the distraught father uttered what many of us feel but hesitate to say, especially to our Lord: "I *do* have faith; oh, help me to have *more!"* (v. 24).

Did you think a Christian has no doubts? Did you suppose a Christian never trembles as he sets out upon an unknown path in faith? Did you think a Christian never wondered whether God was near? Whether God heard him? Had compassion for him? Judged him not?

Oh, my dear fellow Christians, you are a miraculous mixture of faith and doubt—because you are of this world and also of God. It cannot be otherwise; you are made from His breath and the dust of the earth, and God acknowledges this conglomeration. Now it is time for you to do the same.

That is why some doors open and some doors close. That is why some—maddeningly—almost close and keep opening again. There is in your life a constant struggle between your will and the will of God. And He will not overrule you. He endowed you with the freedom to choose, and if He is to have you, He will only have you by your own free choice.

So knock at a closed door. Pound on it until your fists are swollen and bloody. Don't be polite. God does not stand on ceremony.

Raise your voice. Cry out until you are speechless and your throat aches. And then, only then, turn away and seek a door that *will* open to your knocking. There always is one.

Prayer for the Reader

It would be so much easier, Lord, if I could only go through the door You open for me. But You want more from me than unthinking obedience. You gave me the ability to make decisions, and I know You want me to use it. My problem is that I'm afraid to make a mistake or to choose the wrong direction. I forget, sometimes, that even when I go in circles, You are with me. I am never really lost as long as I am with You. So lead me, Lord, beyond the circles and wrong turns into Your Way, because that is where I want to go.

Thy will be done in earth, as it is in heaven.
Mt. 6:10

When You're Lonely

I watch, and am as a sparrow alone upon the house top.
Psms. 102:7

*T*here it is again, the feeling that no one cares, that no one even knows you exist. Where you are has nothing to do with it. You may be in a room filled with people or you may be eating dinner by yourself. You feel cut off. Disconnected. You're lonely.

Loneliness is the child in us, afraid of the darkness of an uncertain world. It is the infant crying out for the parent, longing for the comfort of strong arms around its vulnerable body.

Don't be ashamed of this child in you. It is a wonderful part of yourself. It connects you to God. It brought Jesus to His knees in Gethsemane when He suddenly felt alone among His closest friends. And the child in Him cried out to His Father in Heaven and received the protection of a Parent's presence.

When the child in you cries out, bring it to your Father. Then, when you understand you are truly loved, that you really matter, you will be able to speak to another of your need. And if that other cannot hear you, you will go on to yet another, because you are no longer afraid of being turned away. You know you are lovable.

You know, also, that you have something to give as well as something to ask. When someone else is lonely, you will recognize it. You will understand why that person cannot reach out to you. And you will do the reaching. Your inner child and the other person's child, by clasping hands, will end the loneliness.

Prayer for the Reader
Sometimes I can be standing next to a friend, Father, and feel a great distance between us...sometimes I want to cry out, but have no voice. Only You perceive my uncertain presence. Only You hear the words I cannot bring to my lips. You see me watching You from the roadside, and You reach through the throng to take my hand and bring me close to You. You let me walk with You part of the way, until my step is strong—and then You send me along another road looking for others who have lost their place in the crowd.

Suffer the little children to come unto me.
Mk. 10:14

Lo, I am with you alway.
Mt. 28:20

When You're Envious

You crave for something and don't get it; you are
murderously jealous of what others have got and
which you can't possess yourself.
Jas. 3:16, Phillips

*I*t's an uncomfortable sensation, an uneasy prickle you can't quite locate, a swift tensing of your body, and then —some thoughts you wish you'd never had. Maybe it happened during a conversation with a friend who was sharing good news about her life. All of a sudden the words started forming in your mind: "Why *her*? Why can't something like that happen to me?

Your envy is showing.

And you're ashamed of yourself. You thank God for helping you keep the words to yourself. Nevertheless—you thought them. You resented your friend for a moment; maybe even longer.

Why?

Because your friend's life seemed better than yours?

Because your friend seemed to be getting all the breaks—and you weren't getting any?

Because you think God may love your friend more than He loves you?

Silly, aren't they?

No. Not at all.

These are human feelings. Not our best feelings, but part of the way we're made. Being a Christian doesn't mean we won't be envious. It means we have to deal with the emotion.

An odd thing about envy is that it usually shows up where love is. Or has been. Saul and David, Adam and Eve and God, Joseph and his brothers, the disciples jockeying for first place in heaven,

Paul and the Corinthians—you and your friend with the good breaks. All of them in loving relationships until one person decided that the love wasn't evenly distributed—that one person was getting something the other deserved—that maybe God was playing favorites.

Now we're getting somewhere.

Notice that we usually aren't envious of someone we don't really like. Could it be that in some secret part of ourselves we feel that God doesn't like that person, either? And so, even if something wonderful happens to the person we don't like, we aren't threatened by it. His good fortune doesn't seem to have anything to do with his favor in God's eyes. It's just an accident. Those things happen.

But—someone we like, or admire, or love, that's different. Surely God finds that person lovable, too. More lovable than we are? Possibly. No, that couldn't be! God loves all of us equally.

Except that when I'm down and you're up, when my life is in a shambles and yours is mending, it's hard for me to believe that God loves me as much as He loves you. And, although I'm ashamed to admit it, I *am* threatened by your blessings when mine seem too few.

Why?

Because, like many Christians, I still measure God's love by visible proofs of it. Because, while I may not really believe that the more God loves me, the richer He's going to make me, I am inwardly shaken when a friend prospers and I don't. I become the Prodigal's brother, chafing at his father's embrace of the son who did everything wrong. I become a child, pouting: *I've been good—Why aren't you giving me a big party? Don't you love me anymore?*

That is envy. It preys on the spiritual child in us.

Not that there is anything wrong, or bad, but the spiritual child in us is terrified at the slightest indication that love might be withdrawn. What an ideal environment for the growth and development of envy!

I don't know about you, but I find that the child in me is perfectly happy with my own life when all is going well. That's when a friend—any friend, all friends—can prosper, succeed, be promoted, acknowledged with all kinds of gold medals, and I can share that friend's happiness. My child isn't the least bit threatened. It's only when *I* am having problems that I can't handle *another person's* solutions very well. I feel left out, neglected. *Unloved*. My inner child hurts, and I don't know how to make the hurt go away.

Envy is a sin, there's no denying it. But we can't put a label on it and stop there. Envy won't go away by itself.

When I was a little girl and showed signs of being envious of someone, my elders always told me that I was foolish to think anyone's life was better than mine. If I really knew the other person, I was told, I might find out that he or she had every reason to be miserable. Never mind if the person appeared happy. *You never could tell!*

That kind of advice scared me. Did it mean that if I envied somebody, that person was going to end up unhappy? The truth of the matter usually was that the better I knew the persons I envied, the more enviable their lives appeared to be. Some people's grass really is greener most of the time.

But that is an adult realization, and it doesn't help the spiritual child in us when it feels threatened by a loss of love. And that is what envy is: a fear that we are not cherished, cared for, protected, nourished.

And therein lies an answer to the problem. This child in us needs our attention, our comfort, our assurance of God's love. And it needs that attention right in the midst of its envy.

I have to deal with envy every time I am involved in a typical family scene. It doesn't have to be anything special—just a simple family meal with everyone gathered around. Or a time of crisis when a family closes ranks in support of each other. The sight of a family cheerfully sharing the chores in a laundromat can bring tears of envy to my eyes. I am particularly vulnerable to family living because I missed so much of it. Yet because I do not have a family around me, I am often invited to share the activities of other families.

I can't tell you how many invitations I turned down over several years because I knew how envious I would be if I accepted. I also made a point of spending holidays alone or out of town (also alone). Consequently, I became more and more aware of the fact that I didn't have a family around me. I felt quite sorry for myself, too. Poor me. Lucky others!

Then, one Christmas season when I was planning my annual excuse to get out of all those invitations (and I can't believe how patient my friends were to keep extending them), I ran into a problem. It was going to be especially hard that year because I couldn't afford to go away. In fact, I was very short of money generally and not too optimistic about my future. My spirits couldn't have been lower, and I was throwing the door wide open to resentment toward anyone who seemed to be more fortunate than I was. I decided I wouldn't even have a Christmas tree that year—and I always used to have one, come what might. I wouldn't decorate my house or hang a wreath on the door. Actually I was sulking.

Almost every day I drove past a corner where Christmas trees were stacked in rows. There were trees of all sizes, but one in particular, a small fat one near the curb, kept catching my eye. And I kept turning my head away. No, I would not have a tree that year! I didn't have enough money. Poor me. Nobody cared what happened to me. Especially God.

But that tree stayed near the curb where I could see it. A lot of the other trees were sold, but it seemed that nobody wanted such a small one that year. What a shame. It had such a beautiful shape. I could put it on a table near the window, and at night, when the lights were on, people passing by could see it. I always liked the merry sight of a tree in a window at night.

It was two days before Christmas and I was driving past the corner again. This time I slowed down to get a better look and, sure enough, there it was. A very merry tree, indeed! I pulled over to the curb, parked my car and got out, hurrying to buy that tree before I could say no to myself—that is, if the price was right. The price was perfect; the tree seller was clearly glad to get rid of something no one else wanted.

I can't describe the excitement that was building up in me as I took the tree home and carried it into the house. I felt like a happy child. As I rummaged through the attic for my favorite ornaments, I began to sing Christmas carols out loud.

By the time I decorated the tree, it was dark. I turned on the lights and sat on the floor marveling at their sparkle. Then I realized that I didn't feel the least bit lonely. Or neglected. Or not loved. I felt, in fact, most generously cared for by a God who was especially close to me in those moments. He was sharing my frugalities, rejoicing in my small delights. We were going to spend Christmas together, He and I, and all the days thereafter, the good ones and the lean ones. I was going to worry about what I could do to make ends meet, and He was going to worry right along with me. Together we would explore ways to survive. My world was not nearly as dark as it had seemed when I thought I was alone. Something sparkled in it.

I knew what I wanted to do—and that was to be with people. *With my family*. For I realized that I did have a family after all. My friends, those who wanted me to be a part of their lives, they were my family and I was theirs. We needed to share each other's loaf and two fishes as well as each other's banquets, because what we really were sharing was our regard for each other.

I went to the phone and called the members of my family. "Come and see my wonderful little tree!" I said.

It was short notice for a gathering, but it didn't seem to matter. My house was filled that evening—with friends, with family, with caring.

So what was envy doing in a place like that? It wasn't. Envy was gone.

Prayer for the Reader
It will happen again, Lord. When I'm not looking, envy will slip into my life, and I will pull away from someone I have loved. I'm not trying to make excuses, but sometimes life gets pretty scary. And when that happens, I do feel like a child. Everyone else seems so big and com-

petent and secure, while I seem small, helpless, insignificant. But You understand children. Suffer me to come to You even when I am not particularly lovable. Help me to clear the envy from my eyes by granting me Your vision.

My grace is sufficient for thee.
II Cor. 12:9

Love one another, as I have loved you.
Jn. 15:12

When You Aren't Appreciated

I receive not honour from men.
Jn. 5:41

*D*on't put up with it.
If you can't ever seem to do enough, if you aren't being paid what you are worth, if the credit for your achievements is given to someone else, or none is given at all—if who you are and what you do are taken for granted, don't swallow hard and put up with it. Go to those who will appreciate you.

Not out of spite. Not out of anger or because you are defeated. But out of sensibility. You have an obligation to God and to yourself: God has made you what you are so that He can work through you. You are the channel for His power. But God can't do anything with you or through you if you aren't appreciated.

We're not talking about praise. You are not asking for a medal of commendation. Your self-esteem, bruised as it may be, does not *require* the acclamation of others. But you do need recognition for the person that you are. Your presence in the world, and among those close to you, needs to be acknowledged. A head must nod— yes, you are here, and you are welcome. It's the difference between being called by your name or beckoned with a wave of a hand. Appreciation identifies us as one of God's children.

And if we aren't identified, we become unproductive.

When you aren't appreciated, it's because someone doesn't have faith in you or in your abilities, even though you may have demonstrated them. And it's not your fault. Some people just don't have the capacity to believe.

The important thing is for you to keep faith in yourself, to remember that God created you and you will always have His appreciation. So do what Jesus did when He wasn't appreciated. He went on from there. You need a success experience. Allow God to lead you to it.

Prayer for the Reader
Make me aware, Father, of the others in my life. Help me to look at them in newness and in faith. Give me the vision to discover You in each person. And give me a voice to tell them, in so many words, how much they mean to me.

Neglect not the gift that is in thee.
1 Tim. 4:14

Meeting Life's Demands

To one is given...wisdom, to another...knowledge...to
another faith.
1 Cor. 12:8, 9

When You Have Too Much To Do

I will put upon you none other burden.
Rev. 2:24

*I*t scared me. I had never experienced anything like it. Ever. I felt empty, hollow. I could perceive the world around me and everything in it, but my mind refused to put the pieces together. It refused to think, consider, or care. In fact, my lack of concern was what told me something was wrong. When I *can't* care about my work, about what is happening to my friends and family, then I *know* I'm in trouble.

I was worn out from caring, from doing, from *being*. I couldn't remember the last time I took a day off. My heart still wanted to pull me in six directions at once, but the rest of me just wouldn't go along. I never thought that would happen to me. Why did it?

I think God was sending me a message: STOP!

That's right. STOP! Right in the middle of everything. No, I hadn't finished what I was trying to do. And there wasn't anyone who could take over for me. If the world was going to fall in on me, there wasn't anything I could do about it.

My fear brought me very close to God. Or, rather, it brought Him close to me. And I leaned on Him. I had no choice. I was simply out of giving.

I took the telephone off the hook. I covered my typewriter. I didn't have the energy to put my desk in order. My house was a mess. The laundry wasn't done. I hadn't even thought about dinner. I wasn't hungry. I settled my puppy and cat and then I settled myself in bed. It felt so strange lying there in the daylight. I've never been one to take a nap.

I was too tired to sleep and I lay staring up at the ceiling, its whiteness a welcome blank. I could feel my mind resting, refusing all thoughts that tried to intrude on it. The emptiness in me became so great that I began to cry. I was afraid I would never have any energy again. Could such a thing happen, Lord?

His answer came slowly, over several days. The first thing I felt was a sense of peacefulness filling that terrible emptiness. It was all right to be helpless, it seemed to assure me. It was all right to run out of steam after using too much of it for too long. I was perfectly normal. I remember smiling about that as I dropped off into sleep. In broad daylight.

When I woke up it was dark. My cat was curled up next to me and my puppy's cold nose brushed my cheek lightly. I felt cared for. The burden had been lifted.

I had not fully recovered. But I knew I would. In time. I put myself entirely in God's hands. *If you want me to rest, then I'll find a way*, I promised. *But, Lord I do want my energy back!*

He gave it back a little each day. And one morning I awoke with the zest that was so typical of me. The first thing I did with it was thank God. I'm afraid I was awfully loud about it, but that's how grateful I felt.

I know now that I am as human as you are. Or as anyone else is. I have been blessed with a lot of energy, with marvelous health, and I like to get things done. But I do have my limits, and I ignored that part of my human condition for too long. Finally God had to step in and do something about it. I won't allow that to become necessary again. I know how to rest now—right in the middle of everything. And I discovered something else: the world doesn't fall in on my head when I take a break. It keeps right on turning—because that's His job, not mine.

Prayer for the Reader
No, Lord, I don't want to stop what I'm doing. Nobody gave me these burdens—I put them on myself. I like getting things done. I want to help people. Don't ask me to change—You're the One who made me this way. But

I'm sure You gave me more sense than I've been using. If I'm so good at doing things, then I ought to be able to learn how to pace myself. Thanks for the warning.

They that wait upon the Lord shall renew
their strength.
Isa. 40:31

When You're Ill

And they brought unto him all sick people...and
he healed them.
Mt. 4:24

When we're very young, we almost enjoy being sick. As long as it isn't serious. We become, for a while, the most important person in the world, the center of everyone's attention. Mothers persuade us to eat our favorite foods. Fathers take time to read us stories and press a hand across our forehead before they say good night; everyone definitely becomes more affectionate. Brothers and sisters willingly surrender their fondest possessions; all we have to do is look, longingly. All blame, all wrongs, all sins are wiped out. Our slate is clean. Only we get well.

We almost don't want to get well. Except that being sick gets boring. It still does. Especially when we aren't very young.

Illness can also be frightening to an adult. It comes uninvited, pushing all priorities aside, stranding us in our bed, in our room, or, worse, in a hospital. The rhythmic pattern of every day is totally disrupted, and we are adrift in a sea of uncertainty.

But illness can be a time of exquisite solitude—if we allow God to share it with us. When we are well and vigorous, we savor our own strength, but in the weakness that accompanies illness, we are suddenly aware of God's amazing vitality. It is He reaching out to us now, and if we are very still, we can feel His healing.

Prayer for the Reader
Be my Healer, Jesus. Mend me in mind and spirit as well as body, for I have great need of Your care. Give me patience, revive my hope when it flickers feebly, and build in me such a trust in Your will for me that I will meet each day of my life with the knowledge that I will find in it a blessing.

O Lord my God, in thee do I put my trust.
Psms. 7:1

When You Don't Think
You Have Any Talent

Your labour is not in vain in the Lord.
I Cor. 15:58

"*A*nd what do *you* do?"

It's a tricky question to answer. But not if you have a talent. You can make sense out of computers. You can sing. You can paint, and in fact some of your paintings have been sold, so you *must* be good. You can find out what's wrong with people physically and emotionally. You can make lots of money. You used to be a dancer and now you teach. Your talent is your label. It's what you can tell people you are.

But—suppose you don't think you have a talent? How can you describe yourself? I mean, suppose you can brighten up the dark parts of a room with a touch of color. Or bring a garden to life in a window box high up over a city street. Or you're a person who remembers the important days in other people's lives and you do something about them. Maybe you know what a sick person needs without asking. Or you write newsy letters to friends you don't get to see often. What do you call these things?

They are talents. Every bit as much as an ability that enables someone to rise in the fields of business, art, science or entertainment. Your talents may not make money for you, but they certainly accomplish what a talent is meant to do—which is, to carry out God's work in the world.

So if you are using your talent to make a part of the world a little better for the rest of us, then you're investing it.

That's what *you* do!

Prayer for the Reader

I may be overlooking the talents You gave me, Jesus, the ones that bring me close to people. Kindness, for instance. Understanding. A joy in giving. A sensitivity to unspoken need. Make me aware of these gifts, dear Lord. I think they may be what I need to go with You in Your world.

Let your light so shine before men, that they may
see your good works, and glorify your Father
which is in heaven.
Mt. 5:16

When Everything Seems
To Be Going Wrong

We are troubled on every side.
II Cor. 4:8

*E*verywhere you turn, you meet problems, obstacles, difficulties. Large ones, small ones, all sizes. None of your dreams are coming true. You can deal with disappointment, but not so much of it all at once.

You don't want to say it, but you can't help it—Why? you ask.

Why is this happening to you?

You tell yourself your problems won't last forever. You know you still have some blessings you can count. But—you're tired of looking for solutions. You're tired of being brave. Yet you don't want to complain.

When you hurt, God hurts. Tell Him. It's all right to cry on His shoulder. Tears don't mean you're weak. They mean you feel. And He made you that way.

No, your troubles won't last forever—but what are you going to do in the meantime? Is it possible—just maybe—that you can become a more loving person? Why not? You possess the gift of resurrection!

Do you realize then, what a miracle you are experiencing? In the midst of your heartbreak, your anxiety, your despair, you are being re-created. You are finding qualities of your being that you never knew existed. Don't forget them when the problems are solved. And don't dwell on them when the moments are good—there is no need for that. But the next time you are overwhelmed by misfortunes, you won't have to ask, Why? You'll know you are approaching a time of discovery.

Prayer for the Reader

Father, let the times of testing stretch me—but not so far that I lose touch with You. While I am in this needy condition, lead me into a deeper understanding of others' feelings. Let me not forget the sting of tears so that when I see them in another's eyes I will tend the wound that caused them.

Let not your heart be troubled: ye believe in God,
believe also in me...I will not leave you
comfortless: I will come to you.
Jn. 14:1, 18

When Someone You Love Is Suddenly Taken

The king was much moved, and went up to the chamber over the gate, and wept . . . O Absalom my son, my son!
II Sam. 18:33, NKJV

I knew, the moment I drove down my street, that something was wrong. There were too many cars parked along the curb, and most of them I didn't recognize. Every light in the house next to mine was lit, but there were no sounds of a party. As I pulled into my driveway I wondered if I should ring the Hales' bell and find out what was going on. Then I decided I wouldn't. Something in me didn't want to know.

But I had no choice. The Hales' door opened and I saw Jenny. The expression on her face frightened me. I had never seen such pain.

"Harry's dead!" she said in a whisper that sliced across the lawn.

It made no sense. Harry, the Hales' oldest son, wasn't quite thirty. He was in good health. How could he be dead?

I got out of my car as Jenny came toward me. "He was shot," she said, and her eyes told me that she still couldn't believe it. "Right in front of his apartment. A man walked up to him and shot him and took his watch. Harry's dead!"

I have read of such things. We all have. But it's different when it happens to someone you know. It's suddenly real. And frightening.

"My child is dead," Jenny whimpered. I put my arms around her thin shoulders and held her close, both of us crying. I wanted to say something that would help, but no words came to my mind. Only anger and hatred and a fierce desire for vengeance.

I knew that was wrong. I'm a Christian and I didn't think a Christian should ever feel that way. A Christian should find words of comfort. But where? How? A Christian should do something. What? What can anyone do? Except weep?

It was a long, strange evening for all of us. The Hales' house was filled with friends and family, and none of us knew what to do, what to say. We were choking on our anger, our bitterness, our fear, and feeling guilty because what we really wanted to do was shout out loud at God. But that didn't seem to be the proper way to address God, so we all kept silent. And distant. From each other and from God. We didn't think God would understand what we were going through.

Later, as I lay in the darkness, trying to sleep and not succeeding, I wondered about that assumption of ours. Why *wouldn't* God understand? He knew what violence was. He understood hatred, fear, rage. He saw what they did to His world, and it was into that very world He sent His Son. Jesus walked our streets and felt our fears, and He did it as a human being. He understood, all right. He still does. Yes, we can come to Him in anger, in confusion, or in any of our human ways. Because He will understand.

We can ask Him those questions that torment us: *Why? Why this one I loved? Why someone innocent?* We can beat our fists against His chest and demand a reason for our heartbreak—and His own tears will spill over onto our upturned faces. Yes, He understands. He receives our pain, and weeps—as surely as He wept when John the Baptist was killed. He was there. He knows.

But, no, He will not give you answers to your questions, because none will suffice. Tell me, honestly, is there any answer that will make a difference in your loss? Are there any words that will dry your tears, let you sleep at night, cease your dread of beginning another day without the one you love? Of course not. And that is something you must accept.

There is no replacement for the one you have lost. None. But neither is there vengeance. Turning away from the world will only aggravate the pain and keep you close to it. Resenting the happiness of others who still have their loved ones with them will only keep the death news vibrant, throbbing. You need healing. And there is only one Physician. Let Him care for you.

You will be healed—but there will be a scar. Your life—*you*—will never be the same. How could you be? Someone who was a part of you is gone. But you can go on. And you can give to others what you gave before. Even more. You can give in behalf of the person you lost—just as Jesus gave in behalf of John. You can live, here on earth, for that other and for yourself. God will help you. He is here.

Prayer for the Reader

I am empty, Father. I am bitter, even toward You. I grieve, not only for the one I have lost, but for the loving part of myself that seems to have died as well. You, who have at other times brought the dead back to life, revive my dead ability to love, to be close, to care about this world and those I know. I believe, I insist, that You can heal this mortal wound.

He healeth the broken in heart, and bindeth up their wounds.
Psms. 147:3

When You Lose A Job

For yet a very little while, and the indignation
shall cease.
Isa. 10:25

*H*e was trying to be kind. "You have a lot of abilities," he said. "They just aren't what we need in this job."

I was fired. "It happens to everybody at one time or another," he said, but that didn't help. It had never happened to me and I thought it never would. I had tried so hard to be a good secretary because I needed a job badly. But in all honesty, my typing was terrible—fast, but full of errors. I tried to make up for my lack of shorthand by writing fast—and then I couldn't read what I wrote. In time I might have done better, but I didn't have time.

So I dove into the classified ads. I read every one of them until I knew them by heart. Then one day I found something I thought I could do. A publishing house needed a person who wanted to learn how to edit manuscripts. Beginner okay. At a very low salary, of course. But it was better than nothing.

Yes, I got the job, and I have been in publishing ever since. Obviously it was the right place for me to be. But I wouldn't have known it if I hadn't been fired. And if the man who fired me hadn't been kind as well as honest. I *did* have abilities—we all do—but I wasn't using them in the best possible way. I was trying to fake a talent I didn't have.

Getting fired is a cruel experience and I don't wish it on anyone. Nevertheless, if it happens, it can make a difference if we remember that we are losing a job, not ourselves. No matter what the reason for the job termination, God still believes in us and so should we. Your job ended. *You* didn't.

Prayer for the Reader
You are the only One who can give me sympathy without making me feel sorry for myself, Lord. I need Your tenderness now, but I know You will also give me a shove to get going again. This time, though, I want to rely more on Your sense of direction. I didn't do so well on my own.

Cast not away therefore your confidence.
Heb. 10:35

Shew me thy ways, O Lord; teach me thy paths.
Psms. 25:4

When A Marriage Ends

Let my cry come near before thee, O Lord: give me understanding according to thy word.
Psms. 119:169

*I*t doesn't seem possible that love can die, does it? You remember the vows and the way you felt when you spoke them. *Forever* was something you could feel.

Whoever was at fault, whoever changed, whoever ended it, that's all over. You will have to confront the memories, the shame, anger and sense of failure, but not now. There is something else you have to do first: Think about your life.

Yes, your life. It must go on. Not as it was before. Not even the way it was before you married. This is all new. All different. All very frightening.

But the hurt—what about that? Blows have been exchanged. Wounds inflicted. Pride crushed. All the love, all the care, all the softness you once felt is gone. You're hard, flinty. You've become a weapon poised to strike back.

Is that what you want? Forget about what is fair and what is right. Do you want to worship the god of vengeance? Or the God of love? Do you want to be guided by hate or by compassion? Take your choice.

God isn't going to force you to do anything. If you want to get even, you can justify it. You have your reasons. If you want to spend a good part of your life inflicting pain on someone else, you have that freedom. But you're cutting yourself off from God. Oh, He's on your side. He always will be. But He can't act in hate. He acts in love.

You know what love is. Once, perhaps for a long time, you felt love for the person you now hate. You cared what happened in that person's life. You felt everything he or she experienced as if it happened to you. That won't change. Not entirely. You will feel the pain from any wounds you cause now. Because love doesn't die, even though a relationship may. A part of love remains in you and in the person who shared your life. A small ember of love, perhaps. A bit of regard. But it will always be there. God did join the two of you together, and nothing on earth can totally separate you.

Let kindness be what remains. Let kindness be what you eventually remember long after you rebuild your life. Let kindness be what you take with you. God can help you do that.

Prayer for the Reader
O merciful Father, help me to realize that I am not really a failure. I feel that there is nothing lovable in me. Can You teach me how to care for and love what You have made? You know how—and I want to learn.

Be kindly affectioned one to another.
Rom. 12:10

Answering The Needs
Of Others

*Though I speak with the tongues of men and of angels, and
have not charity, I am become as sounding brass, or a
tinkling cymbal.*
I Cor. 13:1

> *I remember you, The kindness of your youth, The love of your betrothal, When you went after me in the wilderness.*
> Jer. 2:2, NKJV

*T*hey were my ideal couple. Now in their seventies, they had been married for decades. Each one had remained a complete person, fiercely so, and their support of each other came as much out of respect as loyalty. If anyone had asked me, I couldn't have told you which I admired more, Roger or Louise.

But age and illness were taking their toll. First, it was Roger; a serious heart condition that required careful living, a hard task for a man of such mental energy. Then Louise, her spine would never be right again, and she bristled at the prospect of wearing a brace.

I was uncomfortable when I was with them. Gone were their usual lively stands, sometimes on opposite sides of an issue. Instead they were cranky with each other, complaining, obsessed with minor inconveniences. Roger was tired of keeping the house neat while Louise was confined to bed. Louise was all for moving into a retirement community, but Roger wouldn't hear of it. Bicker, bicker, bicker.

And then I saw it—the concern in Louise's eyes when Roger stopped to get his breath. Roger's shaky hand coming down gently over Louise's after she tried once more to get out of bed and couldn't. It was still there: the love. The bliss, the headlong plunge of emotion, the heartbeat flushing the temples, were long since gone. But the commitment was still there.

Commitment. What is this word, *commitment*? I love you with all my heart and mind and soul. Isn't that enough?

No.

Commitment speaks another language. I will not always find it easy to love you, it says. There will be times when I will lose interest in you, when you will annoy me and try my patience. I will even begin to hate you, although I hope those times will not last long enough to destroy our love. We will argue sometimes, you and I, and our differences will not always be healed. We will often be as distant as we are close. I will have to deal with these intrusions on our serenity, our joy in each other, our passion, comfort and devotion—and so will you. At those times love will not always feel like a throbbing heart; it may be very quiet, very steady, but not exactly exciting. But it will be there. That is when love will be at its strongest.

Commitment is Christ in Gethsemane, dreading the pain of love but willing to accept it. It is beauty losing its hair and taking on wrinkles, remembering the bliss, yes, but knowing something more wonderful has grown in its place. It is love daring to live honestly, to meet change, to bear burdens, to gain insights, to trust its own strength. It is an old man's trembling hand on the pain-gnarled hand of his wife; it is her eyes watching his spasm-hunched shoulders.

The falling part is over. Commitment is love with its feet on the ground.

Prayer for the Reader

I want my existence to mean something in the life of another, Lord. I want to care as well as be cared about. That kind of love isn't easy, is it, Lord? Life has so many ways of testing love—dreams that don't come true, broken promises, worry, illness, other loyalties, other attractions, responsibilities. Teach me the kind of love that grows stronger with use.

Walk in love, as Christ also hath loved us.
Eph. 5:2

*Be happy. Grow in Christ. Pay attention to what I
have said. Live in harmony and peace. And may
the God of love and peace be with you.*
II Cor. 13:11, Living Bible

*D*id you ever hear the remark, "Being a parent is the most important job in the world, yet there isn't any course in how to do it"? A comedian said it, meaning it as a joke. But you know it isn't funny.

Everyone tells you it's easier with the second child, but parenthood at any time is an awesome responsibility. Advice? You get too much of it, and all of it different. The best way to bring up a child yesterday is the worst way today.

Suppose you make a mistake? What will that do to your child's future development? Can you discipline your child without turning him or her against you? Are you giving your child enough room to grow? Too much? Are you demonstrating your love? Are you too demonstrative? Are you spending enough time with your child? Or too much? Who can tell you?

You can. And you must.

Like it or not, prepared or unprepared, you are the authority in your child's life. You are not your child's playmate, buddy or best friend. You are your child's guardian, God's delegate in this world. You are your child's guide to reality; the world around your child will be interpreted by you, the parent. You are your child's protector and provider of nourishment. You will receive your child's first uncertain communication; your appreciative response will build in him or her a sense of trust, your attention and encouragement will provide the soil in which his or her self-esteem will grow. Yes, you are important.

If you think that bringing up children is boring, demeaning and a waste of your talents, consider this: You will need, and use, every bit of intelligence, insight, administrative ability, athletic prowess, wit, appreciation of art, music and literature, mechanical engineering, animal husbandry, horticulture, furniture refinishing, typing, home economics, medical know-how and mechanical drafting you have learned or picked up along the way. You will be called to minister to your child's spiritual needs. You will bring God and your child together. There is no more demanding, creative or diversified job in the world than participating in the life of a new and totally unique human being.

But you won't always think so. At times you may be so consumed by your work that you won't be able to see what you are accomplishing. Or it won't seem to matter because you're so tired. Don't think God doesn't understand. He knows what exhaustion is. He knows you need rest. He hasn't put aside your needs because you have a child. And neither should you.

Parenting is not a matter of the hours you put in on the job. Sometimes it isn't a matter of how well you do your job, but that you do it with care. With love. "Short shrift," my great-grandmother used to say when she was trying to take care of me with one hand and doing six other things with the other.

My stepfather was not my biological parent, and at times he must have felt clumsy in the role of my father. At least it seemed so to me. But he cared very much about my well-being. That was particularly evident one Christmas many years ago when my mother was in the hospital recuperating from a long illness. I used to visit her every afternoon after school and my stepfather spent the evenings with her. I would go home, make dinner for myself and get to my homework. When my stepfather came home I always had a glass of milk with him while he ate the dinner I kept warm in the oven.

Although Christmas offered us special hope in a spiritual sense that year, none of us was thinking in terms of Christmas presents. We were just glad my mother was getting well and would soon be home with us. I had bought a gift for each of my parents, but I had no thoughts about a tree or presents under it.

I'll never know how my stepfather found the time to do it, but he managed to gather up a lot of gifts, little ones that didn't cost very much. And he wrapped them most beautifully and put them under the tree. Yes, a tree—which he brought home late on Christmas Eve and decorated from top to bottom. On Christmas morning he tried to make the elaborate breakfast my mother always made for the holidays and he burned most of it. I ate it with tears in my eyes and when I told my stepfather it was delicious, I was telling the truth. We put our gifts into shopping bags and took them to my mother in the hospital. There, like three little children, we tore off the wrappings and opened the boxes.

I have never had such presents! The fleece-lined bright red mittens I had wanted for so long. Thick-ribbed socks, perfect for ice skating. A roll of transparent tape and a holder, to put on my desk. (Very grown-up). A pen. Two handkerchiefs with my initials on them. A classy looking three-ring binder to replace my tattered one—and paper refills! Nothing extravagant. But all of them what I wanted. How did my stepfather *know*? I couldn't remember telling him. Or my mother.

Parents *do* have a way of knowing their children. It comes with the job of being a parent—if we allow God to share our parenting with us.

Prayer for the Reader
As much as my children depend on me, Lord, I depend on You. Give me the steadiness and strength they need when mine runs short.

The Lord will give strength unto his people; the Lord will bless his people with peace.
Psms. 29:11

When A Child Is In Trouble

As Christ forgave you, so also do ye.
Col. 3:13

At first you can't believe it. Not *your* child! You *know* your child would never do something like that!

Then, when you can no longer deny the evidence, you begin to blame yourself for what went wrong. The accusations pile up: You didn't love your child enough. You loved your child too much. You were too easy; too soft. It's all your fault. If only you had—or hadn't....

Stop right there. Do you see what is happening? While you are blaming yourself, your child is the one who needs your attention.

No, your child isn't perfect, not any more than you are. Or anyone else. And this may come as a shock to you. But now you have to face a question: *How* do you love your child? Can you reach out to this frightened young person? Or has your outrage, your shame and your disappointment wiped out that ability? Because at this moment your child needs tangible expressions of your love more than ever before. Not the easy love that springs up from pride in a well-behaved son or daughter. Not the comfortable love that purrs somewhat smugly when you hear about other children getting into trouble. No. This is a hard-to-come-by kind of love that may bring a bitter taste to your mouth. It is nails-piercing-hands love. It isn't earned by a child's perfection, nor is it deserved by obedience. You have to look past the faults to love now, and if you succeed, then you can't even take credit for it. Not really. Because this is the love God has given to you, and it's your turn to pass it on. Oh, yes—

when we talk about loving others as Jesus loves us, that includes our own children.

For many years in my early life, I was one of those model children who never gave her parents a moment's worry. Frankly, I think both they and I were blessed with an amazing amount of good fortune. But then one afternoon my girlfriend and I went roller skating in front of a school a few blocks away, and neither one of us was aware that this was something we weren't supposed to do. There were no signs to that effect. We were having a marvelous time on the smooth broad strip of concrete when suddenly the school door flew open and a custodian roared out. We stood trembling on our ball bearings while he announced to us that no one was allowed to play on school property after regular school hours and he was going to report us to the principal the very next morning. I'll never forget the shame I felt when he took our names, and I tried to imagine what my mother and stepfather would say when they learned that I was a *bad girl*.

I couldn't bring myself to tell them at first. But my parents soon realized that something was wrong because I was just too quiet all evening. Finally they got it out of me. I would be given "a white slip," which was an offical reprimand. My transgression would be entered on my otherwise spotless school record—for all time.

My mother was not a patient woman, and I expected her to react in anger, which she did, but her anger wasn't directed at me. She was indignant at the unfairness of the penalty. If I had known I was breaking a rule, that would be another matter, she said. But there was no way my girlfriend and I could have known.

The next morning my mother was waiting outside the principal's office when he arrived—not to defend me, but to protest the fact that rules were not posted. Later, I was called to the principal's office where he told me the white slip would not be issued. My record was secure. My mother, in her usual haste, aimed a kiss at my cheek, missed, and ran to catch her bus to work.

Well, you can say, I was lucky. I really didn't do anything wrong. But I *felt* as if I had. I *saw* myself as guilty, and later in my life, when I did break some rules, I knew that shattered feeling again. Being wrong, doing something wrong devastates whatever self-esteem we have. But we can repair the damage as long as we know that some part of us is worth the effort. And that is where parents come in.

Prayer for the Reader
How many times, Jesus, have I asked You to be patient with me, to love me in spite of my mistakes? And now my child needs as much from me and may not be able to ask for it. Is my disappointment drowning out his cries for help? Is my own shame preventing him from speaking? I don't want that to happen, Lord. I don't care if I have to shout out loud—I want my child to know how much I love him. Give me Your voice.

By love serve one another.
Gal. 5:13

When A Parent Is Getting Old

I have been young, and now am old.
Psms. 37:25

You notice it in little ways, at first, so it's easy to persuade yourself it isn't happening. For instance, even with her glasses on, your mother has trouble reading the newspaper. But so do you. Sometimes. Going up and down stairs, slowly, tires your dad. More than it should. Or, more than you think it should. You make excuses for crankiness, forgetfulness, long gloomy staring instead of that wonderful smiling disposition. Nobody smiles all the time.

You tell yourself, No, it can't be—your parents aren't old. Why, they're still young by comparison. So are you.

It's hard for any of us to admit that a parent is getting old. The word itself sounds ugly. I know a sprightly man of almost seventy who is totally preoccupied with worry over the health of his mother, who must be near ninety—and who is, indeed, not well. This is a man who prided himself on keeping active, on being at his desk by eight o'clock every morning and putting in a full day's work. He was going to work until he died, he vowed. Now he stays home, helping his wife look after his frail mother.

I can remember the first time I looked at my mother and acknowledged, with a shock, that she was middle-aged. She had always seemed so young and full of energy. Her skin was without wrinkles and her hair without a trace of gray in it, at least, none that I could see. Then one day, all of a sudden, my mother looked different to me. We were riding a bus together and I turned to say something to her. Just then the sunlight coming through the window next to her illuminated what I hadn't seen before. Nothing much, really. A few tiny lines around her eyes and the corners of her mouth. Were they really *gray* hairs wisping at her temple? Or was it the sun playing games in her brown hair? I couldn't speak. I felt frightened, for some reason. I felt exactly the way my almost-seventy friend feels now.

The aging of parents tells us that someday we are going to be without them, and we don't want to be reminded of that. It hurts too much.

It also reminds us that we too must move on, must face a diminishing of our strength and abilities. And somewhere deep inside us is the childlike conviction that a parent is the one person who stands between us and death. Once the parent is gone, we think we have lost that protection and we feel terribly mortal. We know now that we too must deal with death someday.

Does that seem morbid? It can be if we consider death the end of life. But as Christians we know it isn't. Death is a transition time for us. It *is* frightening to think about because we have never been there and we don't know what to expect—in human terms that is. Spiritually we have been well prepared—by the Parent who will never leave us: God Himself. *I will never leave you nor forsake you.* (Hebrews 13:5, NKJV) So old age becomes a preparation time for another part of life. It requires respect, not resignation.

Prayer for the Reader

Lord, help me to grow up a little more as I see my parents aging. It's a difficult time for them—and for me. I need to let go of them just enough so that they are free to move closer to You, but not so much that they feel I have abandoned them. Let me be someone they can lean on when they need strength—but let me also be a grateful recipient of the support they can still provide. I need it, Lord. Let us be leaners, each on the other.

That their hearts might be comforted, being knit
together in love.
Col. 2:2

*B*eing a Christian means that you do not go through life alone. Even in your most solitary moments, God is at your side in the person of His Son and in the presence of His Spirit. You walk with God's hand in yours.

And you will be blessed with the fullest, most meaningful life there is—because being a Christian means letting Christ influence everything you do. It means allowing His personality, His way of thinking, His strength and His tenderness to affect your whole person and all your decisions, relationships, actions and inner life. You don't have to be perfect; you just have to be His.

But don't be afraid to go where He leads you. Don't pull back when you see difficulties ahead. Let Him guide you through them. Let Him hold you up when you are weary. You may get hurt, but He will heal you. If you are anxious, He'll understand and He will tell you about the times when He, too, trembled. Your weakness is not your shame. You are human, and so is He. But He is also divine, and He will share with you the spiritual resources His Father gave to Him. They will bring meaning and purpose to your earthly life—as they did to His.

So let Him take your hand. Let Him teach you the kind of trust, love and obedience that made His life unique. You are God's partner in this world. You are meant to do more than experience this life. You can grow through your experience; you can be strengthened by your struggles. Your own feelings can make you more sensitive to the feelings of others. As you discover your own worth as a human being, your cup will run over and you will pour out of it into the cup of another. This is the way a Christian lives.

> *The Lord bless thee, and keep thee: The Lord make*
> *his face shine upon thee, and be gracious unto thee:*
> *The Lord lift up his countenance upon thee, and*
> *give thee peace.*
> Num. 6:24-26

14 Days

NOV. 1 4 1989
JAN. 2 4 1990
FEB. 8 1990
FEB. 1 6 1990
MAR. 1 2 1990
MAY 2 9 1990
JUN. 5 1990
JUN. 1 4 1990
JUN. 2 5 1990
JUL. 2 1990
JUN. 2 9 1990
AUG. 2 9 1990
SEP. 1 2 1990
SEP. 1 8 1990
DEC. 6 1990
DEC. 3 1 1990
FEB. 2 7 1991
APR 1 2 1991
APR. 1 7 1991
APR 2 3 1991
FEB 2 8 1992
JUN 1 9 1992

JUN 2 9
JUL 2 2 1992
SEP 2 8 1992
JUN 7 1993
JUN 2 0 1994
SEP 1 2 1995
JUN 2 1 1996
MAR 2 1 1997
JUL 1 1 1997
MAY 2 5
MAR 2 1 2000
MAY 3 0 2000
NOV 1 3 2001
JUL 2 9 2002
APR 6 2004
JUL 2 8 '06
JUN 2 5 '07
JUL 2 0 '07
JUL 1 5 '08
AUG 1 5 '08

From Idea
to Toy

From Idea
to Toy

Ali Mitgutsch

 Carolrhoda Books, Inc., Minneapolis

First published in the United States of America 1988 by Carolrhoda Books, Inc.
Original edition ©1987 by Sellier Verlag GmbH, Eching bei München,
West Germany, under the title VOM BÄR ZUM TEDDY.
Revised English text ©1988 by Carolrhoda Books, Inc.
Illustrations ©1987 by Sellier Verlag GmbH
All rights reserved.

LIBRARY OF CONGRESS CATALOGING-IN-PUBLICATION DATA

Mitgutsch, Ali.
    [Vom Bär zum Teddy. English]
    From idea to toy / Ali Mitgutsch.

        p.   cm.
    Translation of: Vom Bär zum Teddy.
    Summary: Describes how a teddy bear is designed and produced.
    ISBN 0-87614-352-4 (lib. bdg.)
    1. Teddy bears—Juvenile literature.   [1. Teddy bears.]
I. Title.
TS2301.T7M6313   1988
668.7'24—dc19   88-22756
                                                          CIP
                                                          AC

Manufactured in the United States of America

1 2 3 4 5 6 7 8 9 10 98 97 96 95 94 93 92 91 90 89 88

From Idea to Toy

Bears look soft and cuddly, but they are strong,
wild animals that are not easily tamed—
unless they are teddy bears!
Teddy bears come in many different
shapes, sizes, and colors.
Artists who work for toy companies design teddy bears.
This artist gets ideas for the teddy bear
she's designing by painting live bears at a zoo.

When she gets home from the zoo,
the artist chooses her favorite drawing.
Using that as a guide, she sketches
every part of the bear separately:
the head, the arms, the legs, and the body.
Each shape is very simple.

The sketches of each body part are sent to a toy factory.

Each sketch is traced onto cardboard and then cut out.

These cardboard pieces are used as patterns.

The pattern is placed on top of some shaggy fabric,

and the body parts of the teddy bears

are cut out of the fabric with scissors.

The pieces of fabric are sewn together to make teddy bear heads, arms, legs, and bodies. Each body part is then sent to another part of the factory.

The head, arms, and legs are joined together.
The shining eyes and the funny little noses
are attached to the bear heads.

The teddy bears are completely assembled,
but they are still hollow.
A machine uses air to blow
foam flakes into each bear.
Now the teddy bears feel soft and cuddly.
They are ready to be carefully packaged
and sent to toy stores all over the world.

Artists have a lot of fun
coming up with ideas for new toys.
But the best part of designing teddy bears
is knowing how happy and excited children will be
when they get one of their very own.

Everyone wants to have a teddy bear.
These loveable toys can go
almost everywhere, even to the park.
Teddy bears can become good friends.

j40433

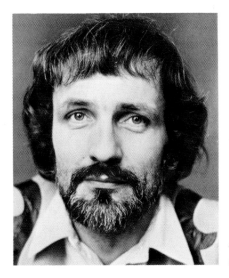

**Ali
Mitgutsch**

ALI MITGUTSCH is one of Germany's best-known children's book illustrators. He is a devoted world traveler, and many of his book ideas have taken shape during his travels. Perhaps this is why they have such international appeal. Mr. Mitgutsch's books have been published in 22 countries and are enjoyed by thousands of readers around the world.

Ali Mitgutsch lives with his wife and three children in Schwabing, the artists' quarter in Munich. The Mitgutsch family also enjoys spending time on their farm in the Bavarian countryside.

THE CAROLRHODA
START

TO FINISH
BOOKS